# Hell Bank
# Notes

## (Contemporary Issues)

## James F. Frayne

**MONTANA PUBLISHERS**

First Printing: 2015

ISBN: 978-1-326-30443-0

Montana Publishers

<u>Ordering information</u>:
Special discounts are available on quantity purchases by corporations, associations, educators, and others.
For details, contact the publisher at the e-mail address detailed below.

<u>U.S. trade bookstores and wholesalers</u>:
Please contact publishers at: e-mail at TGTG2014@hotmail.com

<u>By the same author</u>:
Easy as you Go! A Mathematical Companion (Volume 1: A – L)
Easy as you Go! A Mathematical Companion (Volume 2: M- Z)
A-Star Mathematics Question Bank (Without Solutions)
A-Star Mathematics Question Bank (With Solutions)
Selected Biology Advance Level Topics Volume 1 (A to J)
Selected Biology Advance Level Topics Volume 1 (K to Z))
Tall Grows the Grass (Full Novel)
Tall Grows the Grass (Books 1 – 3)
Jenny Two-tails and her Friends (Children's Story Book)
Romancing the Wood (Wooden Nickel 'Flats' of the USA)
The Indian Hundi (Financial Scrip for Hundreds of Years)
Hidden Stories behind Paper Money around the World

For more details, please visit author's website at http://jamesfrayne.net

# Contents

Preface ……………..……………… 007
Hell Bank Notes ………………...…….. 008
Gallery ……………………………..……. 027

# Preface

It is important to observe that the reference to "Bank Notes" in no way infers that any of the notes in this publication have been produced by an Issuing Bank. It would be completely wrong to infer this in any way.

These notes are *faux notes*, as such they are not an officially recognized currency or legal tender since their sole intended purpose is to be offered as burnt-offerings to the deceased as often practiced by the Chinese and several East Asian cultures. their specific purpose being to be burnt in strict accordance with Taoist tradition.

They therefore more rightly belong to the category of '**Exonumia**' under the branch of **fantasy notes**.

Even so, because of their strong underlying tradition and the symbolism contained within most of them, they remain of great interest.

It is with this spirit that images of most of the contemporary examples are presented here. Mainly from China, but also other countries as well. This is not, however, an exhaustive collection of images insofar as new ones are being produced (and burnt) all the time. It is hoped that a future revision of this publication will include many more issues of this interesting genre of fantasy notes.

James F Frayne
2015

# Hell Bank Notes
# 地獄鈔票

Hell bank notes are a form of joss paper printed to resemble bank notes.

This *faux money* has been in use since at least the late 19th century and possibly much earlier.

Early 20th century examples took the resemblance of minor commercial currency of the type issued by businesses across China until the mid 1940s.

Hell bank notes are not an officially recognized currency or legal tender anywhere in the world, as their sole intended purpose are burnt-offerings to the deceased as often practiced by the Chinese.

The identification of this type of *joss paper* as "hell bank notes" and singling them out is largely a western phenomenon, since these items are simply regarded as yet another form of joss paper (冥幣, 陰司紙, 紙錢, or 金紙) and have no special name or status.

Earlier examples of these notes were issued in denominations of $5 and $10 yuan and upwards, with such amounts being considered adequate until inflation took hold within China from 1944.

地獄紙幣是一種形式香燭紙打印到類似鈔票。

這種人造錢已在使用中至少自19世紀後期，可能要早得多。

早在20世紀的例子採取了相似的小型商業貨幣的類型發出業務遍布中國，直到20世紀40年代中期。

地獄鈔票不是一個官方認可的貨幣或法定貨幣在世界任何地方，因為他們唯一的預期目的是燔祭死者經常練的中國人。

該識別這種類型的冥鏹為"地獄鈔票"和挑選出來，主要是西方的現象，因為這些項目簡單地視為又一形式冥鏹（冥幣，陰司紙，紙錢，或金紙）並沒有特別的名稱或狀態。

前面的例子，這些票據發行的面額為 500和$ 10元以上，金額等被認為是足夠了，直到通貨膨脹率從 1944年在中國舉行

The soaring denominations of
authentic currency was soon reflected
in that issued for the afterlife, and
after 1945 the many Hell banknotes
were issued in denominations of $10,000 or higher.

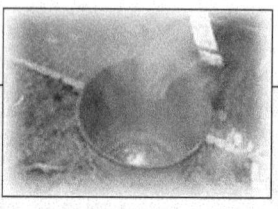

These earlier issues more commonly depict landscape scenes,
temples or trains, and the numerous varieties may literally number
into the millions.

Modern Hell bank notes are known for their large denominations,
ranging from $10,000 to several billions, and usually bear an
image of the Jade Emperor, the presiding monarch of heaven in
Taoism, with his signature (Romanized as *Yu Wong*, or *Yuk
Wong*) and the signature of *Yanluo*, King of Hell (閻羅).

There is usually an image of the Bank of Hell on the back of the
notes.

The word *hell* on hell bank notes refers to *Diyu* (simplified
Chinese: 地狱; traditional Chinese: 地獄; pinyin: *dìyù*, meaning
"underworld prison"), which is also called dìfǔ (Chinese: 地府;
meaning "underworld court"). These words are printed on some
notes. In traditional Chinese beliefs, it is thought to be where the
souls of the dead are first judged by the Lord of the Earthly Court
(*Yan Wang*). After being judged they are either escorted to
heaven or sent into the maze of underground levels and chambers
to atone for their sins. People believe that even in the earthy court,
spirits need to use money.

面額的暴漲的真實貨幣很快就體現在頒發的來世, 和
1945年以後的許多地獄紙幣發行了面值1萬元或更高。

這些早期的問題較為普遍的場景描繪風景, 寺廟或火車,
和眾多的品種, 從字面上電話號碼以百萬計。
現代地獄鈔票是眾所周知的大面額, 從 1萬元至數十億
美元, 而且通常承擔著形象的玉皇大帝, 主持會議的君
主天道教, 與他的簽名(羅馬的禹皇, 或育王)和簽名的
燕羅, 閻王(閻羅)。
通常會有一個形象的銀行地獄背面的說明。

這個詞在地獄地獄鈔票是指迪宇(簡化中國:地獄, 傳統
中國:地獄;拼音:迪宇, 意思是"黑社會監獄"), 這也叫
dífǔ (中國:地府, 意思是"黑社會法庭")。這些話都印
上一些筆記。在中國傳統的信仰, 它被認為是其中的靈
魂是死是第一評判主的地支法院(燕王)。經過判斷他們
要么護送到天堂或送入地下迷宮水平和商會要為他們
的罪孽贖罪。人們相信, 即使在土場, 精神需要用錢

A story says that the word *hell* was introduced to China by Christian missionaries, who preached that all non-Christian Chinese people would "go to hell" when they died, and through a case of misinterpretation, it was believed that the word "Hell" was the proper English term for the afterlife, and hence the word was adopted.

However, some printed notes omit the word "hell" and sometimes will replace it with "heaven" or "paradise". These particular bills are usually found in joss packs meant to be burned for Chinese deities. They usually have the same design as hell bank notes but with different colours.

A commonly sold hell bank note is the $10,000 note that is styled after the old United States Federal Reserve Note. The front side contains, apart from the portrait of the Jade Emperor, the seal of the Hell bank. The seal consists of a picture of the Hell bank itself. Many tiny, faint "Hell Bank Notes are scattered on the back in yellow. These are sold in packs of 50 to 150, and are wrapped in cellophane.

Some bills do not portray the Jade Emperor, and portray other famous figures from Chinese mythology instead, such as the Eight Immortals, the Buddha, Yama, or images of dragons. Some even portray famous people who are deceased, such as US President John F. Kennedy, Albert Einstein and Marilyn Monroe.

Despite looking like play money, hell bank notes are taken seriously by many people. There are several customs and taboos regarding their proper usage.

有一個故事說，這個詞地獄傳入中國的基督教傳教士，誰鼓吹所有非基督徒中國人會"下地獄"，當他們死了，並通過案件的誤解，有人認為這個詞"地獄"是正確的英文術語為來世，因此這個詞獲得通過。

然而，一些印刷紙幣省略單詞"地獄"，有時將其替換為"天堂"或"天堂"。這些特殊的法案通常在香包旨在為中國神被燒毀。他們通常具有相同的設計，地獄的鈔票，但用不同的顏色。

一個經常賣地獄鈔票是1萬美元的注意，是風格老後美國聯邦儲備局注。正面包含，除了肖像的玉皇大帝，密封的地獄銀行。印章包括圖片銀行自身的地獄。許多微小的，淡淡的"地獄銀行注"S分散背面為黃色。這些銷往包50到150，並包裹在玻璃紙。

一些法案不刻畫玉皇大帝，和其他著名人物刻畫，從中國神話相反，如八仙過海，菩薩，閻王，或圖像的龍。有人甚至描繪著名的人誰是死者，如美國總統約翰肯尼迪，阿爾伯特愛因斯坦和瑪麗蓮夢露。

儘管看上去像打錢，地獄鈔票是認真對待許多人。有幾個方面的禁忌習俗和正確使用。

It is highly offensive in all Chinese communities to give a hell bank note to a living person as a gift. When burning the notes, the notes are placed as a loose bundle, in a manner considered respectful. Alternatively, in some customs, each bank note may be folded in a specific way before being tossed into the fire because of the belief that burning real money brings bad luck.

While custom of burning hell bank notes is legal and still commonly practiced in China, more extremes of this practice of burnt offerings for the deceased, which includes *"luxury villas, sedan cars, mistresses and other messy sacrificial items..."*, according to the Ministry of Civil Affairs in 2006, will be subject to ban due to what is described as feudal superstition.

*Chinese Hell Note from 1940s*

這是非常反感的所有中國人社區給予了地獄鈔票到一個活生生的人作為禮物。當燃燒的音符，票據都放在一個鬆散的捆綁，尊重的方式考慮。另外，在一些海關，各銀行注意可能被折疊在一個特定的方法之前，扔到火，因為相信燒真錢帶來壞運氣。

雖然自燃燒地獄的鈔票仍是合法的和普遍實行的中國，這種做法更加極端的燔祭的死者，其中包括"豪華別墅，轎車，包二奶等祭祀物品凌亂…",根據在民政部於 2006 年，將受到禁止因什麼被描述為封建迷信。

# Four Guardians of the Four Compass Directions
## Celestial Emblems of the Chinese Emperor
Chinese: 四神, Pinyin: Shishin

| | |
|---|---|
| **Tortoise (Black Warrior)** | = North, Winter, Black, Water |
| **White Tiger (Kirin)** | = West, Fall, White, Metal |
| **Red Bird (Phoenix)** | = South, Summer, Red, Fire |
| **Dragon** | = East, Spring, Blue/Green, Wood |

At the heart of Chinese mythology are four spiritual creatures (Sì Shòu 四獸) - four celestial emblems - each guarding a direction on the compass.

In China, the four date back to at least the 2nd century BCE. Each creature has a corresponding season, colour, element, virtue, and other traits. Further, each corresponds to a quadrant in the sky, with each quadrant containing seven *seishuku*, or star constellations (also called the 28 lunar mansions or lodges). Each of the four groups of seven is associated with one of the four celestial creatures.

There was a fifth direction - the centre, representing China itself - which carried its own *seishuku*. The latter four are the Buddhist guardians of the four directions who serve *Lord Taishakuten* (who represents the centre), and are closely associated with China's Theory of Five Elements.

| 四監護人四大羅盤方向富徵記的中國皇帝 |
|---|

| | | |
|---|---|---|
| 龜(黑武士) | = 北方, 冬季, 黑色, | |
| 水白虎(麒麟) | = 西, 秋季, 白, | |
| 金屬紅鳥(鳳凰) | = 南, 夏, 紅, | |
| 火龍 | = 東方, 春, 藍/綠, 木 | |

在心臟的中國神話的四靈動物（四獸）- 四個天體標誌 - 每個守著一個方向的指南針。

在中國，四，至少可以追溯到公元前2世紀。每個生物都有一個對應的季節，色彩，元素，美德和其他特徵。此外，每個對應一個象限中的天空，每個象限包含七個 seishuku，或星星座（也稱為28個月球豪宅或旅館）。每個四組七是與一個四天體生物。

有第五個方向 - 中心，代表中國本身 - 載著自己 seishuku。後四是佛教監護人的四個方向誰擔任主 Taishakuten（誰代表中心），並會密切與中國的五行理論。

## Chinese animal symbolism

**Lion**
Although China is not an indigenous home for lions, the lion is visible everywhere. Some art historians believe that the image may have arrived in China during the time of ancient Egypt and Mesopotamia. Since lions have never been a real danger in China, their symbolic function has emphasized their protective powers. Lion images can be suitable and effective as protectors of the fame and reputation of the individual or family.

**Tiger**
The tiger is also featured prominently in Chinese mythology and ranks second behind the lion as a badge of military rank. Tiger images can give us the audacity to go forward with new ventures.

*Lion* 獅子

中國動物象徵

獅子
雖然中國是不是原家獅子，獅子是隨處可見。一些藝
術史學家認為，圖像可能已抵達中國的時間在古埃
及，美索不達米亞。因為獅子從來就不是一個真正的
危險在中國，他們的象徵功能強調其保護的權力。獅
子圖像可以適當和有效的保護的知名度和聲響的個人
或家庭。

虎
老虎也是中國神話中佔有突出地位，居第二位，僅次
於獅子作為徽章的軍銜。虎圖像可以給我們大膽往前
走新的合資企業。

*Tiger* 虎

**Birds**
The Chinese are highly fond of birds, and the range of climate in China is so extensive that practically every family of birds is represented. For this reason, the symbolic importance of birds is also wide-ranging.

The crane is well known as the bird of happiness.
The goose is supposed to mate for life and both geese and ducks serve as symbols of fidelity and conjugal bliss.
The peacock symbolizes dignity, beauty and official rank.
The dove and pigeon are revered for their devotion to their young.
The swallow is a general bird of good omen and fortune.

**Tortoise**
Supernaturally endowed with amazing powers, tortoises are emblematic of steadfast effort and eventual, inevitable success.

*Eagle* 鷹

鳥
中國人非常喜歡鳥，並在中國範圍內的氣候是如此廣泛，幾乎每一個家庭的鳥類的代表。出於這個原因，在象徵意義的鳥也廣泛。

起重機是著名的鳥類幸福。
該鵝應該是隊友的生命，都鵝鴨作為象徵忠誠和偕老。
孔雀象徵著尊嚴，美麗和官階。
鴿子和鴿都尊敬他們奉獻自己的青春。
燕子是一般的鳥的好兆頭和財富。

龜
超自然賦予了驚人的力量，是象徵龜的堅定努力，最終，必然成功。

*Tortoise* 龜

**Dragon**
A symbol of the emperor himself, the dragon was master of all of the elements of nature. The sinuous dragon can take many forms and can be victorious in any circumstance. A pregnant dragon is particularly auspicious as a symbol of future growth and expansion. The dragon is most useful in connection with fame, reputation and career.

**Phoenix**
The phoenix, the second outstanding mythical beast, was traditionally associated with the Chinese empress, but was available for use by all women. The phoenix, an enormous winged bird, dwells immortally in the highest regions of heaven. The phoenix comes to earth to presage great events for mortals. The phoenix can be used as a symbol of the accomplishment of a formidable task or the building of a lasting monument.

*Dragon* 龍

龍
象徵著皇帝本人，龍是掌握所有的元素的性質。在蜿蜒的巨龍可以採取多種形式，可以在任何情況下取得勝利。懷孕龍是吉祥的象徵，特別是對未來的增長和擴張。龍是最有效的連接與名望，聲譽和事業。

鳳凰
鳳凰，第二個優秀神話野獸，傳統上與中國的皇后，但可使用的所有婦女。鳳凰，一個巨大的鳥翼，dwells不朽的最高地區的天堂。鳳來到地球，預示著偉大的事件為凡人。鳳凰可以作為一個符號的成就是一項艱鉅的任務或建設一個持久的豐碑。

*Phoenix* 鳳凰

# Chinese Flowers

**Chrysanthemum** 菊花
The Chrysanthemum signifies a life of
ease. Symbolic of powerful Yang energy,
this flower is an attractant of good luck.

菊花象徵生命的緩解。楊符號的強大能量，這花是一個
引誘的好運氣。

**Citron** 檸檬
Citron stand for luck and happiness. It is
known as the Buddha's hand because the
upturned petals of the Citron are reminiscent
of the upturned fingers of the Buddha's
meditative position.

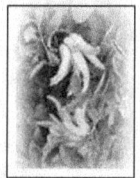

柚子代表幸運和幸福。它被稱為佛手，因為上翹花瓣的
雪鐵龍是讓人聯想到上翹手指佛冥想的位置。

**Hydrangea** 繡球
A symbol expressing love, gratitude, and
enlightenment. Due to it's versatility, and
beauty, the hydrangea makes an excellent
thank you gift to an unsung hero in our lives.

符號表達愛，感恩，和啟迪。由於它的多功能性和美感
，使一個優秀的繡球感謝你的禮物到幕後英雄在我們的
生活。

### Lotus 蓮花

The Lotus symbolizes ultimate purity and perfection because it rises untainted and beautiful from the mud. Every part of the plant, from roots to petals can be put to good use and has medicinal properties. As such, the plant as a whole, conveys deep significance. It represents inward emptying and outward splendour.

蓮花象徵著純潔和完美的，因為最終它上升污點和美麗的泥漿。每部分的植物，從根部到花瓣能善加利用，並具有藥用性質。因此，該廠作為一個整體，傳達深刻的意義。它代表排空向內和向外的輝煌。

### Narcissus 水仙

This flower is said to bestow the flowering of our hidden talents. It is reputed to augment the hard work put into careers, assuring those with careers will be rewarded when incorporating this auspicious symbol in their lives.

據說這種花開花賜給我們的隱藏的人才。它是馳名的辛勤工作，以增加投入的事業，保證那些事業會得到回報的時候加入這種吉祥的象徵，在他們的生活。

## Orchid 蘭花

The Orchid is a symbol of perfection, abundance, and higher growth, when we focus on the endless loveliness of this flower we are able to open the flow of exotic beauty and prosperity in our lives.

蘭花是一種象徵完美，豐富和較大幅度的增長，當我們著眼於無盡的可愛的這個花，我們可以打開流外來的美麗和繁榮我們的生活。

## Peony 牡丹

The Peony is a symbol for nobility and value. It became popular in the imperial palaces during the Sui and Tang dynasties, and earned the title of the "king of flowers". A symbol of spring, it is also used as a metaphor for female beauty. In full bloom, the peony symbolizes peace.

牡丹是一個符號為貴族和價值。它成為流行的皇宮在隋唐時期，贏得了冠軍的"王花"，一個象徵春天，它也被用作比喻女性的美麗。盛開，牡丹象徵著和平。

GALLERY

畫廊

50 dollars

15.0cm x 7.5cm

Serial Number 1249

The Chinese dragon on
the left hand side facing
left.

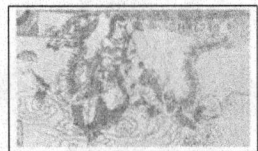

On the right Yu Huang
appears and is accompanied by a vase of flowers.

More flowers are seen on both sides on the
reverse of the note.

On the reverse the are two tigers
embracing a dragon guilloche.

0 dollars

0.0cm x 0.0cm

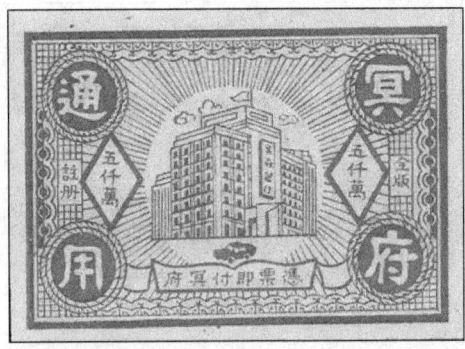

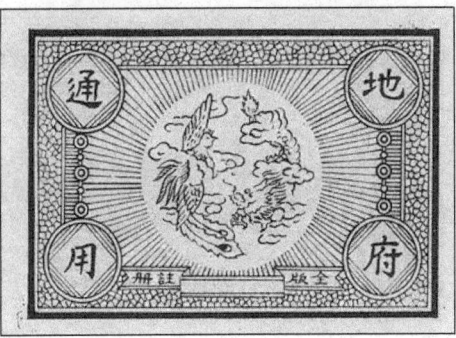

0 dollars

0cm x 0cm

# 1

1 dollar
15.5cm x 6.5cm

# 1

1 dollar
12.8cm x 6.2cm

# 1

1 dollar
15.5cm x 7.5cm

# 1

1 dollar
15.4cm x 7.5cm

# 1

1 dollar
15.5cm x 7.6cm

**2**

2 dollars
15.9cm x 7.1cm

# 2

2 dollars

13.5cm x 8.2cm

# 2

2 dollars
15.5cm x 7.5cm

# 2

2 dollars
12.7cm x 5.8cm

# 2

2 dollars
15.5cm x 7.6cm

# 2

2 dollars
12.8cm x 6.2cm

# 5

5 dollars
15.9cm x 7.1cm

# 5

5 dollars
13.2cm x 6.4cm

# 5

5 dollars
14.2cm x 7.3cm

# 5

5 dollars
15.5cm x 7.5cm

# 5

5 dollars
14.9cm x 6.7cm

# 5

5 dollars
15.3cm x 7.4cm

# 5

5 dollars
15.5cm x 7.6cm

# 5

5 dollars
13.2cm x 6.4cm

# 10

10 dollars
17.3cm x 8.3cm

# 10

10 dollars
13.5cm x 6.2cm

# 10

10 dollars
13.5cm x 6.5cm

# 10

10 dollars
15.9cm x 7.1cm

# 10

10 dollars

13.5cm x 6.7cm

# 10

10 dollars
15.0cm x 7.6cm

# 10

10 dollars
14.5cm x 6.7cm

# 10

10 dollars
15.5cm x 7.5cm

# 10

10 dollars
15.3cm x 7.3cm

# 10

10 dollars
15.5cm x 7.5cm

# 10

0 dollars

15.5cm x 7.6cm

# 20

20 dollars
15.3cm x 7.6cm

# 20

20 dollars
15.5cm x 7.5cm

# 20

20 dollars
15.6cm x 6.5cm

# 20

20 dollars
15.6cm x 6.5cm

# 50

50 dollars
15.0cm x 7.5cm

# 50

50 dollars
15.9cm x 7.1cm

# 50

50 dollars
15.3cm x 6.9cm

# 50

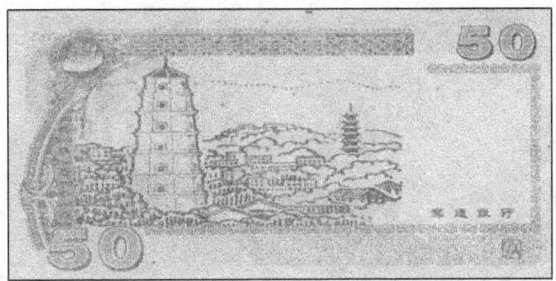

50 dollars
17.3cm x 8.3cm

# 50

50 dollars
14.9cm x 6.8cm

# 50

50 dollars
15.5cm x 7.6cm

# 50

50 dollars
15.3cm x 7.5cm

# 50

50 dollars
16.9cm x 7.6cm

# 50

50 dollars
15.3cm x 7.0cm

# 50

50 dollars
15.5cm x 7.5cm

# 50

50 dollars
15.5cm x 7.5cm

# 50

50 dollars
15.5cm x 7.6cm

# 50

50 dollars

15.5cm x 7.6cm

# 50

50 dollars
15.5cm x 7.5cm

# 50

50 dollars
15.6cm x 6.5cm

# 50

50 dollars
15.3cm x 7.5cm

# 50

50 dollars

15.6cm x 7.5cm

# 50

50 dollars

15.6cm x 6.5cm

# 80

80 dollars
15.3cm x 7.5cm

# 100

100 dollars
15.6cm x 6.5cm

# 100

100 dollars
42.4cm x 18.8cm

# 100

100 dollars
15.5cm x 7.5cm

# 100

100 dollars
15.5cm x 7.5cm

# 100

100 dollars
15.4cm x 7.6cm

# 100

100 dollars
15.5cm x 7.5cm

# 100

100 dollars
17.4cm x 8.2cm

# 100

100 dollars
15.0cm x 7.0cm

# 100

100 dollars
15.0cm x 7.0cm

# 100

100 dollars
15.5cm x 7.7cm

# 100

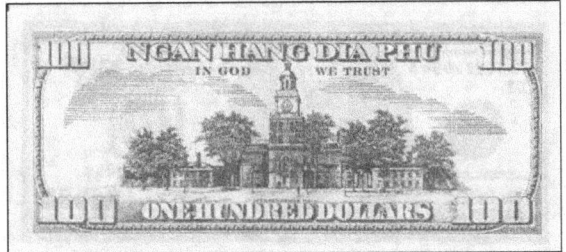

100 dollars

15.4cm x 6.4cm

# 100

100 dollars
15.4cm x 6.4cm

# 100

100 dollars
14.7cm x 7.3cm

# 100

100 dollars
15.5cm x 7.6cm

# 100

100 dollars
14.9cm x 7.3cm

# 100

100 dollars
15.3cm x 7.5cm

# 100

100 dollars
15.3cm x 7.5cm

# 100

100 dollars
19.0cm x 9.5cm

# 100

100 dollars
14.7cm x 7cm

# 100

100 dollars
16.8cm x 7.2cm

# 500

500 dollars

15.5cm x 7.5cm

# 500

500 dollars
15.5cm x 7.6cm

# 500

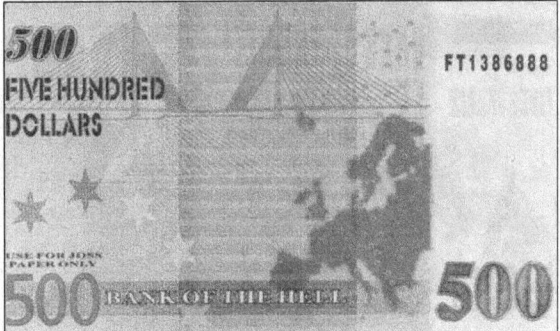

500 dollars

15.5cm x 7.7cm

# 500

500 dollars

15.3cm x 7.5cm

# 500

500 dollars

15.3cm x 7.5cm

# 500

500 dollars
17.3cm x 8.4cm

# 500

500 dollars
15.5cm x 7.7cm

# 500

500 dollars
17.5cm x 8.5cm

# 500

500 dollars
16.7cm x 7.7cm

# 500

500 dollars
14.5cm x 7.0cm

# 1,000

1000 dollars
15.2cm x 8.6cm

# 1,000

1,000 dollars
15.3cm x 6.5cm

# 1,000

1,000 dollars
15.5cm x 7.6cm

# 1,000

1,000 dollars
15.5cm x 7.5cm

# 1,000

1,000 dollars

15.4cm x 7.5cm

# 1,000

1,000 dollars
15.2cm x 7.3cm

# 1,000

1,000 dollars
15.5cm x 7.6cm

# 1,000

1,000 dollars
14.9cm x 7.2cm

# 1,000

1,000 dollars
15.3cm x 7.5cm

# 1,000

1,000 dollars
15.3cm x 7.5cm

# 1,000

1,000 dollars
14.7cm x 7.2cm

# 5,000

5,000 dollars
15.3cm x 7.5cm

# 5,000

5,000 dollars
15.3cm x 7.5cm

# 5,000

5,000 dollars
15.6cm x 6.5cm

# 10,000

10,000 dollars

15.0cm x 6.5cm

# 10,000

10,000 dollars
15.0cm x 6.5cm

# 10,000

10,000 dong
12.9cm x 6.1cm

# 10,000

10,000 dollars
15.6cm x 6.5cm

# 10,000

10,000 dollars
15.6cm x 6.5cm

# 10,000

10,000 dollars
15.6cm x 6.5cm

# 10,000

10,000 dollars
15.9cm x 7.6cm

# 10,000

10,000 dollars
15.5cm x 8.6cm

# 10,000

10,000 dollars

152cm x 8.6cm

# 10,000

10,000 dollars
15.5cm x 6.5cm

# 10,000

10,000 dollars
15.3cm x 7.5cm

# 10,000

10,000 dollars
15.3cm x 7.5cm

# 10,000

10,000 dollars
15.3cm x 7.5cm

# 10,000

10,000 dollars
15.3cm x 7.5cm

# 10,000

10,000 dollars
15.6cm x 6.5cm

# 10,000

10,000 dollars
0cm x 0cm

# 10,000

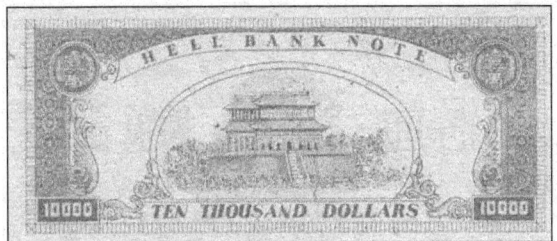

10,000 dollars

15.6cm x 6.5cm

# 20,000

20,000 dong
12.9cm x 6.2cm

# 50,000

50,000 dong
15.3cm x 6.5cm

# 50,000

50,000 dollars
15.5cm x 7.6cm

# 80,000

80,000 dollars
15.3cm x 7.5cm

# 100,000

100,000 dollars
11.8cm x 6.3cm

# 100,000

100,000 dollars
11.8cm x 6.3cm

# 100,000

100,000 dollars
11.8cm x 6.3cm

# 100,000

100,000 dollars
11.8cm x 6.3cm

# 100,000

100,000 dollars
11.8cm x 6.3cm

# 100,000

100,000 dollars
11.8cm x 6.3cm

# 100,000

100,000 dollars
11.8cm x 6.3cm

# 100,000

100,000 dollars
11.8cm x 6.3cm

# 100,000

100,000 dong
15.3cm x 6.5cm

# 100,000

100,000 dollars
15.6cm x 6.5cm

# 100,000

100,000 dollars
15.5cm x 7.5cm

# 100,000

100,000 dollars
15.5cm x 7.5cm

# 100,000

100,000 dollars
15.3cm x 7.5cm

# 200,000

200,000 dong
15.3cm x 6.5cm

# 500,000

500,000 dong
15.3cm x 6.5cm

# 500,000

500,000 dong
15.5cm x 6.5cm

# 1M

1,000,000 dong

0cm x 0cm

# 1M

1,000,000 dollars
18.0cm x 9.6cm

# 1M

1,000,000 dollars

15.3cm x 7.7cm

# 1M

1,000,000 dollars
18.5cm x 9.7cm

# 1M

1,000,000 dollars
15.3cm x 7.5cm

# 5M

5,000,000 dollars
11.8cm x 6.5cm

# 5M

5,000,000 dollars
12.5cm x 6.5cm

# 5M

5,000,000 dollars
13.7cm x 6.8cm

# 10M

10,000,000 dollars
15.5cm x 7.7cm

# 10M

10,000,000 dollars
24.0cm x 11.7cm

# 10M

10,000,000 dollars
17.5cm x 10.0cm

# 10M

10,000,000 dollars
17.7cm x 7.7cm

# 10M

10,000,000 dollars
20.6cm x 9.2cm

# 10M

10,000,000 dollars

19.0cm x 9.5cm

# 10M

10,000,000 dollars
18.5cm x 9.7cm

# 20M

20,000,000 dollars
18.5cm x 9.7cm

# 50M

50,000,000 dollars
19.0cm x 8.2cm

# 50M

50,000,000 dollars
17.5cm x 9.9cm

# 50M

50,000,000 dollars
18.0cm x 9.6cm

# 50M

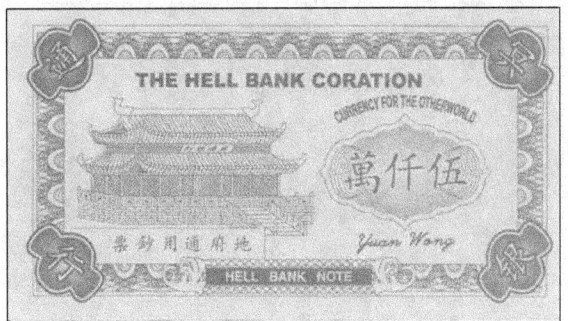

50,000,000 dollars

18.0cm x 9.6cm

# 50M

50,000,000 dollars
11.1cm x 5.5cm

# 50M

50,000,000 dollars

0cm x 0cm

# 50M

50,000,000 dollars
15.3cm x 7.5cm

# 50M

50,000,000 dollars
0cm x 0cm

# 50M

50,000,000 dollars
0cm x 0cm

# 50M

50,000,000 dollars
18.5cm x 9.7cm

# 50M

50,000,000 dollars
18.5cm x 9.7cm

# 50M

50,000,000 dollars
15.3cm x 7.5cm

# 50M

50,000,000 dollars
15.5cm x 7.7cm

# 100M

100,000,000 dollars
15.5cm x 7.7cm

# 100M

100,000,000 dollars
19.0cm x 8.9cm

# 100M

100,000,000 dollars
19.0cm x 10.7cm

# 100M

100,000,000 dong
0cm x 0cm

# 200M

200,000,000 dollars
19.0cm x 8.9cm

# 300M

300,000,000 dollars
18.5cm x 9.7cm

# 500M

500,000,000 dollars
18.6cm x 10.1cm

# 500M

500,000,000 dollars
19.0cm x 8.9cm

# 500M

500,000,000 dollars

18.6cm x 10.2cm

# 800M

800,000,000 dollars
16.9cm x 8.8cm

# 800M

800,000,000 dollars
15.3cm x 7.5cm

# 800M

800,000,000 dollars
19.0cm x 9.5cm

# 800M

800,000,000 dollars
19.0cm x 9.5cm

# 800M

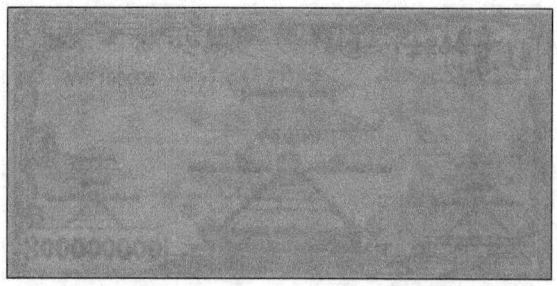

800,000,000 dollars
19.0cm x 8.9cm

# 800M

800,000,000 dollars
17.0cm x 9.5cm

# 800M

800,000,000 dollars

18.9cm x 9.5cm

# 1B

1,000,000,000 dollars
24.0cm x 12.5cm

# 1B

1,000,000,000 dollars
0cm x 0cm

# 1B

1,000,000,000 dollars
0cm x 0cm

# 1B

1,000,000,000 dollars
15.3cm x 7.5cm

# 1B

1,000,000,000 dollars
20.5cm x 11.0cm

# 1B

1,000,000,000 dollars
21.9cm x 11.5cm

# 1B

1,000,000,000 dollars
20.0cm x 10.6cm

# 1B

1,000,000,000 dollars
19.0cm x 9.5cm

# 1B

1,000,000,000 dollars

18.9cm x 9.5cm

# 1B

1,000,000,000 dollars
23.2cm x 12.0cm

# 1B

1,000,000,000 dollars
19.0cm x 8.9cm

# 1B

1,000,000,000 dollars

0cm x 0cm

# 2B

2,000,000,000 dollars
0cm x 0cm

# 2B

2,000,000,000 dollars
19.0cm x 8.9cm

# 2B

2,000,000,000 dollars

24.0cm x 14.2cm

# 2B

2,000,000,000 dollars
18.9cm x 9.5cm

# 2B

2,000,000,000 dollars
19.0cm x 9.5cm

# 5B

5,000,000,000 dollars
19.0cm x 8.9cm

# 5B

5,000,000,000 dollars

25.4cm x 10.6cm

# 8B

8,000,000,000 dollars
19.0cm x 9.5cm

# 8B

8,000,000,000 dollars
18.9cm x 9.5cm

# 8B

8,000,000,000 dollars
32.5cm x 15.5cm

# 10B

10,000,000,000 dollars
0cm x 0cm

# 10B

10,000,000,000 dollars
37.5cm x 21.0cm

# 10B

10,000,000,000 dollars
19.0cm x 8.9cm

# 10B

10,000,000,000 dollars
18.9cm x 9.5cm

# 20B

2,000,000,000 dollars
21.8cm x 12.7cm

# 20B

20,000,000,000 dollars
26.5cm x 15.3cm

# 1T

1,000,000,000,000 dollars
0.0cm x 0.0cm

# 1T

1,000,000,000,000 dollars
19.0cm x 9.5cm

# 1T

1,000,000,000,000 dollars
37.7cm x 17.4cm

Also available from the same author:

ISBN:
978-1-326-79351-7

This book represents a mere selection of the Wooden Nickel 'Flats'
that have been issued since the late 1930s. Even just this small
selection, though, uncovers a wealth of local history. Yet to uncover
all this information nation-wide would mean volume after volume of
incredible history.

Available through all major book sellers including
Amazon as a paper-back in black & white or Kindle in
full colour.

Also available from the same author:

ISBN:
978-1-326-87077-5

What makes Hundis so interesting is the sheer variety of them and the uses to which they were put. As a safety precaution, moreover, they were usually written in an elaborate script which only bankers knew how to read and write. They are still used in India today, even though the resources of modern banking are available for most commercial transactions.

Available through all major book sellers including Amazon as a paper-back in black & white or Kindle in full colour.

Also available from the same author:

ISBN:
978-0-244-60232-1

The note that gave the game away for a fleeing monarch; notes that
were printed with a child's John Bull printing set; notes that were
issued during times of siege; the Government that was involved in
gun-boat diplomacy, forgery and illegal drug smuggling. The notes
involved and many more, together with the illuminating stories
behind them, are all in this publication.

Available through all major book sellers including
Amazon as a paper-back in black & white or Kindle in
full colour.

www.ingramcontent.com/pod-product-compliance
Lightning Source LLC
Chambersburg PA
CBHW060454290526
45791CB00001B/113